Edwards 11.7.11.7.

M. ♩ 76

L. Wayne Updike, 1955

Franklyn S. Weddle and Evan A. Fry

1. With a stead-fast faith to - geth-er let us walk As we seek our Fa-ther's mind;
2. With a stead-fast faith to - geth-er let us walk That the sons of earth may know
3. With a stead-fast faith to - geth-er let us walk, Serv-ing with a com-mon heart,

In our dai - ly task, and in his word re-vealed His e - ter - nal pur-pose find.
The a-bun-dant life, the way his Son has taught, And in Christ-like stat - ure grow.
Shar-ing grate-ful-ly the Spir - it's con-stant care And to all his love im - part.

Words and music used by permission of the author and composer.

Kendra

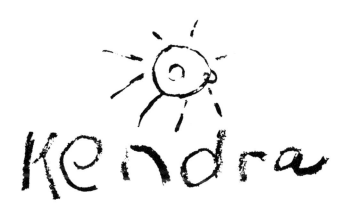

Kendra

**By Gretchen Booz
and Reed M. Holmes**

Copyright © 1979
Gretchen Booz

All rights in this book are reserved. No part
of the text may be reproduced in any form
without written permission of the publishers,
except brief quotations used in connection
with reviews in magazines or newspapers.

Library of Congress Cataloging in Publication
Data

Booz, Gretchen.
  Kendra.

    1. Consolation. 2. Booz, Gretchen.
I. Holmes, Reed M., joint author. II. Title.
BV4907.B62   248´.86   79-12285
ISBN 0-8309-0234-1

Printed in the U.S.A.

FOREWORD

Rarely is death so agonizing for the living as it is when a small child is the victim of a fatal accident. Kendra was such a victim. One moment vitally present; the next moment, gone.

That was twelve years ago. From then until now numerous parents have turned to Kendra's father and mother, Don and Gretchen Booz, for the comfort which can be given best by those who have suffered through grief to a most unlikely resolution of joy.

For the sake of many who know already, or will yet experience such heartbreaking loss, I finally gathered the courage to ask Gretchen to share her story as the mother of that beautiful little girl, Kendra, who had captured our hearts as neighbors. The first three chapters were written by Gretchen. To her testimony are added my own words spoken at the funeral. We hope that this small volume will ease the hurt which so many share.

Reed M. Holmes

TO ALL PARENTS

"I'll lend you for a little time
    a child of mine," He said,
"For you to love the while she lives
    and mourn for when she's dead.
It may be six or seven years,
    or twenty-two or three.
But will you, till I call her back,
    take care of her for me?
She'll bring her charms to gladden you and,
    should her stay be brief,
You'll have her lovely memories
    as solace for your grief.

"I cannot promise she will stay,
    since all from earth return,
But there are lessons taught down there
    I want this child to learn.
I've looked the wide world over
    in my search for teachers true,
And from the throngs that crowd life's lanes
    I have selected you.
Now will you give her all your love,
    nor think the labor vain,
Nor hate me when I come to call
    to take her back again?"

I fancied that I heard them say,
    "Dear Lord, Thy will be done!

For all the joy the child shall bring,
    the risk of grief we'll run.
We'll shelter her with tenderness,
    we'll love her while we may,
And for the happiness we've known,
    forever grateful stay.
But should the angels call for her
    much sooner than we've planned,
We'll brave the bitter grief that comes
    and try to understand.''

—Edgar Guest
(adapted by Ed Closson)

THE LORD IS NIGH UNTO THEM THAT ARE OF A BROKEN HEART.

—Psalm 34:18.

The setting sun cast an orange glow across the water of Nisswa Lake, Minnesota, that Saturday evening in July. Our vacation was drawing to a close, and we were packing in preparation for our return home to Missouri.

Eleven of us had made the trip to Minnesota—Don and I with our two children, Kendra (one week from her sixth birthday) and Joe (two years of age); my parents, aunt, uncle, and three cousins. It had been a disappointing week since rain and 35-degree weather had forced us inside and prevented us from enjoying fishing, boating, swimming, and building sand castles with the children on the beach. Instead, we played games, dramatized proverbs, popped popcorn, and sang songs. Singing made Kendra the happiest. She had just completed a week in vacation church school back home in Independence and had learned the hymn, "With a Steadfast Faith Together Let Us Walk." Many times each day, she would request to sing *her* song. With such sweetness she would stand erect as though performing for a whole congregation of people and would sing all three stanzas of it.

As the sun began to set, the men decided to take advantage of the one evening of pleasant weather we had experienced on the lake and attempt to catch some fish. They untied the boat from the dock and began to drift into the lake as the remainder of our group took the children and started toward the village shopping center. We were going to buy a few items for a quick breakfast which would ready us for a long day of traveling.

We approached the divided highway, crossed the east-bound lane, and were standing in the median strip waiting for traffic to clear before we proceeded across. I carried little Joe and glanced behind me to be sure Kendra was safe. She was standing between my mother and my aunt, grasping their hands tightly. Someone remarked that we should stop for an ice-cream cone. Suddenly there was a terrible screeching of brakes immediately to our right, and as I turned quickly I saw my mother and Kendra rolling down the highway from the impact of an automobile. I ran to Kendra, dropped to my knees with such force that the skin was torn from them, and scooped her into my arms. I had worked six years as a medical assistant in a neurosurgeon's office and was knowledgeable about proper treatment for injured persons. But the concern and despair which I felt for my child at that moment overcame that knowledge, and I did not recall it until someone shouted to me, "Lay her down."

Within seconds, a large crowd gathered. Don and my father came running from the lake, and immediately we drew together in prayer for strength. A nurse arrived and told me that my mother was dead but kept assuring me that our daughter would be all right. I clung to her words in the ambulance as we made the twelve-mile trip to Brainerd Hospital. Don and I prayed together that the Lord would not let our little child die.

Upon arrival at the hospital, Kendra was taken into the emergency unit while Don and I were left standing beside my mother's body in the corridor. Within minutes the doctor approached us with the news that Kendra, too, had expired. Shock, disappointment, and bitterness overcame me and I walked out a nearby door and sat down on the sidewalk. I cried out in extreme anger, "God, *why* did you let this happen?" Instantly a power flooded my body until I felt I could not contain it. I was pulled from that sidewalk with a tremendous surge of strength. I tried to interpret to Don what I was feeling: "Honey, surely this means that we should go to Kendra and pray. There are no elders of the church near for laying on of hands and the prayer of faith. It is up to us." I remember that Don displayed strength unequal to any I had seen in my lifetime.

As we approached the door of the room where our little girl was, a Catholic priest intervened and blocked the doorway. He inquired as to why we wanted to go into the room. We explained to him the experience which I had just had on the sidewalk and we wanted to spend a few moments in prayer with our daughter. The priest stepped aside and allowed us to enter the room. As we stood over Kendra, Don prayed an inspired prayer of submission, placing our precious child back into the hands of the One who had blessed us with the gift of her life. As Don closed his prayer, a radiant glow surrounded Kendra's face. She had never looked more beautiful to us. Now the meaning of the experience on the sidewalk was clear. . . . The Lord *is* "nigh unto them that are of a broken heart," and he does save us when our spirits are crushed! He gave me strength to withstand that which was before me.

We invited the Catholic priest into the hospital chapel where family members were united in prayer for one another—especially for my father who suddenly found himself without his companion of thirty-eight years and his granddaughter who was so very, very close to him.

As we left the chapel, I noticed a handsome, well-dressed young couple sitting in the hospital waiting room; the man was holding his head in his hands. He was the driver of the car which had struck and killed my mother and child. Just before the accident, he and his wife had been sipping martinis in a supper club waiting to be served dinner. They decided to make a quick trip to the motel to check on the safety of their children before eating dinner. They were returning to the restaurant when they met us on the highway. With reflexes dulled and vision blurred, he veered off the highway, striking mother and Kendra. As he sat on the sofa in the hospital, he didn't raise his head. I walked past him and out the door.

Upon our return to the resort, Joe was placed in my arms. A woman whom we did not know had taken him from the scene of

the accident to her home where she rocked
him on her lap until we returned. I held him
tightly as Don and I explained that Sister had
gone to live with Jesus. He seemed to sense
this before we explained. Little did we realize
at that moment the tremendous faith Joe
had even before the age of three and the
enduring strength which he would lend us in
the years to come.

We walked into our cabin and my eyes fell
upon Kendra's doll which she had placed on
her pillow to await her return from the shopping center. The thought that her tender
arms would not cuddle the doll again
brought anguish. On the table were rocks
placed in a straight row. Kendra had
gathered the choicest ones from the beach
and tried to keep them wet by dabbing them
with a moist cloth. "They are so much
prettier when they are wet," she said.
Beside the bed were the little patent leather
shoes of which she was so proud (she
always wanted them tied so tightly that her
feet would soon ache). On a plate were the
remains of a peanut butter and jelly
sandwich I had prepared as a special favor
because she was hungry for her favorite
treat. All of these things brought a feeling of
emptiness which cannot be expressed in
words. Where could we turn for something

to take away our terrible pain?

Don opened the Scriptures and read aloud as Dad, Joe, and I lay upon our beds. Oh, how we grasped every word of the promises contained there. All our lives we had read these scriptures, but tonight for the first time they were speaking directly to us as if they had been written specifically for this moment of our dire need.

We read on. Never before had the inspired words held such meaning — insight into paradise, the resurrection, the promise of "all things being restored to a proper and perfect frame." How important and comforting they were, and how they eased the deep hurt!

We felt fortunate to have the knowledge of the promises contained in the scriptures, but we knew it was going to take daily courage to apply those promises to our future. C. S. Lewis once said, "When pain is to be borne, a little courage helps more than much knowledge."

Could we bear this pain?

Would happiness ever again be restored to our lives?

Would music, which was so much a part of our family, be enjoyed without our favorite little vocalist?

How courageous were we?

WHAT WE HAVE ONCE ENJOYED
WE CAN NEVER LOSE.

All that we love deeply becomes a part of us. — Helen Keller

The initial stage of shock was beginning to pass, and the second day I felt intense grief. My arms literally ached to hold Kendra. There were times when I felt if I could only run a great distance my body would some-how be relieved of the pain which it bore.

I was bothered by the fact that our daughter was unable to have the blessing of administration* at a time in her life when she needed it most. She had been miraculously healed twice. While we were living in Ohio, the doctor's care and medication seemed to be ineffective, and her condition worsened until she was seriously ill. As Don left for the drugstore with a new prescription, I knelt beside her bed. In great concern, I presented her to God. As I walked from her bed, she jumped to her feet and followed me to the kitchen. Her strength was restored and the

---

*An ordinance of the church, mentioned in the Scriptures: "Is any sick among you? let him call for the elders of the church; and let them pray over him, anointing him with oil in the name of the Lord; And the prayer of faith shall save the sick, and the Lord shall raise him up."

illness a thing of the past. As a result of such experiences, Kendra had great faith in the power of prayer.

God had displayed his love for Kendra and she had walked very closely with him. Now, at her death, I asked myself, "Was her life less important than the life of the daughter of Jairus Christ raised from her deathbed?" Christ himself led us to believe that great works are possible for his followers. Was this scripture speaking to me? Was resurrection possible for Kendra? I wondered if it was radical thinking to consider that God might be expecting me to exercise the fullest amount of faith which I could muster. Would I someday meet the Master face-to-face and hear him say, with all compassion, "Gretchen, if only your faith had been stronger"? These questions continued to plague me, and I presented them to Don for his reaction. I approached Don with the idea of the elders administering to Kendra when her body arrived via plane from Minnesota. He was understanding and suggested that I discuss it with one of our ministers. I located him and asked for his guidance. Through discussion and counsel, I decided that this was not the proper thing to do. In analyzing my request, I realized it was very selfish of me to want to bring Kendra back from a place where she was free from sorrow and hurt.

From this point I felt that I had finally submitted her totally to God. Don had done this in the emergency room at the hospital in Minnesota, but it took me two days to finally let go.

We found no comfort in asking "why" nor in dwelling on the thought, "If only we had done things differently that night this wouldn't have happened." It *had* happened, and our mutual desire now was to take this severe loneliness and pain and turn it into constructive living. But the hurt was so deep that it seemed impossible to go on without Kendra.

She was such an important part of us. She came into our lives eleven months after our marriage at a time when our relationship was strained. Each of us was putting petty, selfish issues ahead of the type of marriage companionship which God had intended for us and which we had mutually vowed to build. Kendra came as an angel with a mission to unite us. She did just that. Now with her mission accomplished, she had returned to her heavenly Father.

But how could I live each day without her fun-loving spirit. . .her candid witness of her friend, Jesus. . .the love which she expressed so generously...the close companionship which she and I felt when Don traveled in his work from Monday through Friday each week. We would go from my grown-up kitchen to *her* playhouse kitchen where she served pretzels and punch...and sometimes an imaginary five-course meal. We had fun together! She would lie at my feet while I rocked Joe, or she would squeeze into the small space on the edge of the chair. Together we sang songs and made up stories that would take us on wild, imaginary journeys. Many of these stories and songs were recorded; her whole personality was projected into each tale she told and each song she sang. Such a creative, joyful, talented little girl!

Kendra was sensitive to the needs of others. Following a presentation by Charles Neff regarding the children in India, Kendra went to work. She chose a hot summer day to set up her business in our front yard. She cut out paper bookmarks in the shape of a cross, colored them brightly, and sold them for three cents apiece. Pitcher after pitcher of lemonade went out our door that day. The neighbors patronized her stand, and at the close of the day she had five dollars for the needy children in India. That money now waited in a box on her dresser.

It was impossible for this precious and important child of God to be eliminated from our thoughts, our dreams, and our day-by-day living. We would not even *try* to do so!

There were well-meaning friends who encouraged us to immediately destroy all material things which were Kendra's possessions. Others insisted that we acquaint ourselves with the word "dead" and face the fact that our child was now in that state. Another felt God had taken Kendra as punishment for something we had done and urged us to make a fuller commitment to him.

We rejected these philosophies. This was not the positive, constructive thinking which we needed at this time. We saw no reason to accept the word "dead" in relationship to Kendra. We chose to hold onto the scriptures that say:

> *He that liveth and believeth in me*
> *shall never die.*
> *I am the resurrection and the life.*
> *O death, where is thy sting? O grave,*
> *where is thy victory?*

Viewed apart from Christ, fear and defeat are valid. But through the resurrection of Jesus, we knew our Kendra had stepped from this life into paradise where she would continue her work for the sake of the kingdom of God.

We can *never* lose our Kendra....She is deeply a part of us!

THE DEEPER THAT SORROW CARVES INTO YOUR BEING, THE MORE JOY YOU CAN CONTAIN.

—Kahlil Gibran

There was a very special person in Kendra's life who lived up the street a few houses. She sensed a quality in his life that brought great feelings of happiness when she was in his presence. I recall one time when she and I were in the large, empty Conference Chamber at the Auditorium and Kendra exclaimed, "Mommie, there *he* is!" I didn't know who "he" was, for I saw only a man in a plaid shirt at the back of the Auditorium. As she started running to him, and he walked toward her, I recognized it to be Reed Holmes. He swept Kendra into his arms, and they shared a few minutes in conversation which was just between them. She loved him! This was indeed a special relationship that only Reed and Kendra completely understood.

As Don and I sat down to make plans for the funeral service there was no discussion as to who would present the message. It was just understood between us that it should be Kendra's special friend. When we called Reed, who was in Iowa at the time, he informed us that he was well into the preparation of the sermon, sensing that the responsibility would be his. God poured out his Spirit upon Reed and directed his creative talent so that he was able to greatly minister to our family. He lifted us to levels of joy as we envisioned with him "*our* child going forth."

We felt hope, joy, and love as another friend sang Kendra's song, "With a Steadfast Faith Together Let Us Walk." This was her message to us during the week before her death, and it shall always be her message to us. An artist at Herald House designed a plaque with these words, and it hangs on our kitchen wall. "WITH A STEADFAST FAITH TOGETHER LET US WALK" is the Booz family motto. Many times it causes tears to flow as we sing the song in various settings, but they are tears of joy because it unites us with our Kendra.

Following Kendra's service we went to Des Moines for my mother's funeral. Those days were demanding both physically and emotionally, and we felt fatigued as we returned to our home. As we pulled into the driveway I glanced at the long row of creeping phlox which bordered the retaining wall in our yard. The phlox had bloomed in

April, and we had taken a picture of Kendra sitting beside the beautiful display of flowers. Now, in July, the blooming season was past and the border was green foliage. When I stepped from the car I noticed two blossoms side by side in the center of the border. My soul thrilled at this evidence of renewed life before me; these two blossoms signified to me that Kendra and Mother continue to live. I photographed the flowers, picked them, and pressed them in my Bible beside the words of Christ recorded in John: "Because I live, ye shall live also."

The feelings of joy were sporadic at first, but each day I found new joy through a loved one or friend who allowed me to talk about Kendra. My sister, to whom I have been very close all my life, lived one block away from me at this time. She listened patiently, and I knew she felt every emotion that I was feeling. How important it was to have someone outside our immediate household who deeply cared and understood the periods of adjustment which I was passing through—someone who planned things to stimulate my interest in activity and who would not allow me to draw inward in my grief.

One morning I was alone in our home. Don had left for work, and Joe was still sleeping. It was the week of Kendra's birthday, and the man from the bicycle store had just picked up the purple bicycle which we had purchased before going to Minnesota. It was hidden very carefully under blankets in the garage so it would be a surprise on her sixth birthday. Loneliness seemed more than I could bear, and I sat down on the sofa to cry. Joe awoke and appeared on the stairs in his pajamas. "Why are you crying, Mommie? Jesus is going to bring Kendra back, and it might be today!" He had such hope in his voice and such radiance in his little face! A two-year-old had just given me the strength I needed for that day and for many more to follow. I answered, "You're right, Joe, it *might* be today!"

I often kept myself going for Joe's sake. Even a two-year-old child grieves in the event of death. At times he would hide himself under the drapes; he just wanted to be left alone. There were days when he felt Don would not return from work: Kendra didn't come back, so maybe Daddy would not return either. Don would leave his office and return home to reassure him. We tried to lead Joe gently through a healthy grieving period so the emotion which he was feeling would be expressed openly.

Two weeks after the funeral Joe presented a special request. We had just finished our prayers and were tucking him into bed when he looked at us and asked, "Can I have a baby brother or sister?" Less than ten months later—and after only fifteen minutes at the hospital— we had our new little Katie. I shall never forget the tears which rolled from Dr. Harry Jonas' eyes, down his cheeks, and over his mask as this miracle of birth took place. He had sat with us in our home ten months earlier after the accident and there were tears of sorrow. But tonight, as Katie was born, the tears which were shed by all of us were tears of joy! Joy was greater because of the deep sorrow which had previously carved into our beings! The beautiful baby girl with which God blessed us was not a replacement for Kendra. No, Kendra could never be replaced. Katie was sent to us to fill the void in our family with her own unique talents and personality. Oh, how she was loved and ap- preciated! Upon introduction to her brother at home, Joe took her in his arms and said, "She's mine!" Yes, she was Joe's—he needed her!

We found we were not alone in sorrow and pain. All around us there were people crying for ministry to help bring them through trials. Because we had experienced grief, we were better able to understand the heartaches of others. The responsibility continues to be ours to reach out in compassion and understanding to help others regain real joy. We have found joy and challenge as Kendra's short life continues to affect our priorities. What memories we have of her—and what a future with her!

4

Words Spoken at the Funeral of
KENDRA

You may be familiar with a rather remarkable poem by Walt Whitman. It seemed appropriate, and I have taken the liberty of adapting it:

There was a child went forth every day,
And the first object she look'd upon,
*   that object she became*
And that object became part of her....

The early lilacs became part of this child
And grass and white and red morning-
*   glories, and white and red clover, and*
*   the song of the bird*
And the lambs...and fish...and water
*   plants, all became part of her...*

As did the school mistress...and the
*   friendly, or quarrelsome boys*
And the tidy and fresh-cheek'd girls...
And all the changes of city and country
*   wherever she went.*

Her own parents, he that had father'd
*   her, and she that had conceived and*
*   birth'd her—*

*They gave the child more of themselves
    than that
They gave her afterward every day, they
    became part of her.*

*The family usages, the language, the
    company, the furniture, the yearning
    and swelling heart,
Affection that will not be gainsay'd,
    the sense of what is real. . . (and so
    much more). . .*

*These became part of that child who
    went forth every day, and who now
    goes, and will always go forth every
    day.*

This place will never be the same again,
nor will our neighborhood, nor will the Booz
household. This is not a complaint, although
it is spoken with heartache. It is rather a
tribute to one of the tiniest of the angels.
Because she is gone, the place is strangely
empty, though it is full.

In the death of a little girl, the truth expressed by John Donne is crystal clear:
"Weep not for whom the bell tolls—it tolls
for thee." Each one of us has suffered a
mortal blow. In moments like this we know
we are linked together. We feel it in the ache

of shared loss, and in the wretched realization that we or ours could be next.

This death, of course, strikes us as particularly tragic. She was so young. I suppose all of us have thought of this, again and again. We could border on bitterness about it; it seems so unfair.

And it is unfair, like every other death that rudely comes too soon.

The alternative, of course, would be to schedule death for each of us. We know intuitively that this would not be an improvement. Most of us would prefer to live with the uncertainty and the freedom of not knowing when our time will come.

But we cannot help rebelling against the death of a small child of such obvious promise.

Some will offer an easy answer: "It was God's will." I do not believe that at all. It is too easy. It not only makes God a scapegoat for our unexplainable tragedies; it takes away from us the responsibility to alter our way of life to conform to his will, and not to use it as an easy excuse. Such an answer makes God the perpetrator of violence, and one who uses people as instruments of his violence, thus destroying both the violent and the innocent.

No, this was not the intentional will of

God. I am sure of that. But at the same time, I believe God is not taken by surprise, and that he can and does take our tragedies as they come, helping us to turn them to the achievement of his will.

God is prepared for our tragedies. He demonstrated this at Calvary where crucifixion was turned to victory—and that seemed most unlikely indeed.

I know this will trouble some, for it has been simple to dismiss tragedy with a stoic, "It was God's will." But it leaves us with a jaundiced view of the mercy of a God who traffics lightly in human suffering. No wonder many have been turned away from the "will of God"!

He does not hurt in order to heal. He heals because we are hurt.

Yes, she left early, but when is the proper time to leave family and friends? Only for a very few is life counted out as three score and ten years.

How do you measure life?

In the counting out of years? Then Kendra scarcely lived at all.

In possessions stacked so high? Then she was poor, for there were no years for accumulating.

In skills and dexterity? The tiny fingers were not yet sure of paintbrush and pencil.

The customary measures may not be so valid after all. Oh, this is not to decry long life, or wealth, or skill — nor all that fills life out with creativeness and happiness. Rather it is to say that life's true measure is frequently obscured, and that Kendra may help us to get our bearings.

The dimensions of her life seem very small until we count those who were won by that winsome personality.

Add the diminsion of remarkable sensitivity to others and to relationships between people.

Add the magnitude of her sense of wonder about life.

Add the discernment which was beyond her years.

Add the generosity of love which she poured out to many of us.

Add the radiant smile.

Add the joy.

A life can be full without being big or long, and sure it is that a bud may be more perfect than a flower in full bloom.

Instead of supposing that so many years are due to us, we would do better to figure the length of life as being from birth to death, and pack these moments with the kind of cargo and meaning which is worthy to endure. Then the mystery of abundant or eternal life can unfold even now.

* * * * * *

I do not know the length and breadth of heaven, or whatever better place God has reserved for such as Kendra. I cannot describe to the crossing of t's or the dotting of i's what relationships and conditions shall prevail beyond death. But this I know — that God who is disclosed to us in Jesus, the Galilean, is one in whom we can put our trust.

Jesus did not spend a great deal of time describing what lies beyond death; he simply and wonderfully conquered death and showed to us what men had not seen so clearly before — that it is possible for us all to move from death to life, rather than just from life to death.

Jesus left the definite impression that what people had seen in his life made the victory possible. What they saw there was truth and courage and anger at wrong. Most of all, what they saw was love that was sympathetic enough to weep with those who mourned and gentle enough to nestle a child in his arms.

If these be accurate expressions of the Father who sent him, what is to be feared?

To such a one, Kendra has gone. No one will feel more at home in the arms of the

Galilean. No one will be more willing to make room for another who needs his love. They will understand each other very well.

* * * * * *

I remember the spontaneous smile, the eager greeting (sometimes so eager that she ran), the sharing of wonders, and small wounds, and tidbits of information.

In my case, the way to Kendra's heart was paved by my baby-sitting daughter. I was "Jewell's daddy" long before I became Reed in my own right. I know how my family has been crushed, and I know this is shared by many. The heartache has helped us all to understand a bit how Don and Gretchen feel.

I have regrets that may be typical of others' regrets. Having a privileged spot, why didn't I stop more often to pass the time of day with one who was absorbed with wonders that I hardly ever take time for anymore?

Indeed, if the truth be known, most of us spend too little time with our children. I admit this to my chagrin and thank Kendra for reminding me once again.

Failure to spend more time with Kendra is now past, and to dwell on it, or to cultivate guilt feelings of any kind, or to think what might have been if this. . .or this. . .or this. . .would be beside the point. "Where do we go from here?" is the question. What kind of persons are we to be who have known the touch of her tiny hand?

To mention her name, to recall something about her, to see things about the house that are constant reminders, these may bring pain for a while. But they are not to be avoided. And soon, by some mystery of love, memory will turn from anguish to a means of blessing and motivation.

And one thing more. Those who were nearest to Kendra will find that their loves have been deepened, even by the suffering. They will be able to bring a ministry of understanding and comfort to others who are in the anguish of bereavement, or some other kind of trouble. Don and Gretchen, you are called to this ministry.

Some fleeting snatches of scripture come to mind with particular appropriateness:

Suffer little children to come unto me, and forbid them not, for of such is the kingdom of heaven.
Sorrow not as those who have no hope.

The most mysterious, and in many ways the most wonderful of all, was one that greeted my eyes each morning when I was a child:

All things work together for good to them that love God.

There have been times when that promise seemed unlikely as it was put to the test, but it is true.

* * * * * *

Kendra — the child who went forth every day, and who now goes, and will always go forth every day!